Design
Sourcebook

STAINED
GLASS

FIGURATIVE DESIGNS

I**N THEIR FIGURATIVE WORK**, stained glass artists may take inspiration

from many sources – for example, people, nature, architecture or mythology.

Their designs may be symbolic or realistic. The human figure, fish,

flowers and birds, whether stylized or realistic, can be the essence

of the design or may be depicted in small details which may be as

fascinating to gaze upon and as beautiful as an entire window.

◣ **The Curse of Blodeuwedd II.** Gareth
Morgan. Painted and leaded. 22 ¼ x 30 ¾ in
(56 x 77 cm). 1994

*This beautiful panel was inspired by a
Welsh myth in which a girl changed into
an owl. The irregular outline was deliberately
created to capture the drama of her
extraordinary metamorphosis.*

▷ **Two Angels.** Gaylene Allan-Richardson.
Painted and leaded. Overall size: 22 in (56 cm)
square. 1996

*Though the artist has used vibrant colours in
this piece, she nonetheless retains the gentleness
of the imagery with complementary shades. The
subtle and graceful form of the larger angel is
highlighted in the simple outline and
background of the dark paintwork.*

For ease of reference, we have organized the book thematically, so it is possible to compare the variety of approaches by different artists to similar subjects. We have included imaginative subjects for windows in both domestic dwellings and public buildings, in addition to a selection of autonomous panels which function as works of art in their own right, as well as being the personal expression of the artist.

Space was necessarily limited, and since it was desirable to show as many details as possible, we may have placed a close-up view of a subject under a heading for which the overall concept or inspiration may have been much broader. Some artists may, understandably, find these themes restrictive, but I am sure they will understand the rationale.

Finally, I would like to thank all the contributors for their assistance in the making of this book which, I believe, demonstrates clearly the unparalleled beauty and limitless potential of stained glass.

LYNETTE WRIGLEY

INTRODUCTION

THE REVIVAL IN POPULARITY of stained glass has brought about a renaissance in the approach to its design. Contemporary artists are turning the centuries-old tradition of painted and leaded windows into a modern art form. Their fresh and innovative designs are creating a new image for stained glass, contributing to an appreciation of a medium that is now increasingly being used in both domestic and public settings.

Comprising an invaluable portfolio of contemporary work by artists from Europe, North America, Japan and Australasia, this design sourcebook demonstrates clearly how contemporary stained glass artists are experimenting with the unique attributes of the medium. It contains a wealth of ideas to inspire and encourage students, artists and designers for whom glass offers exciting possibilities for creativity. In addition, it will act as an invaluable guide to the work of different artists for those

seeking to commission an original window or autonomous panel.

CONTENTS

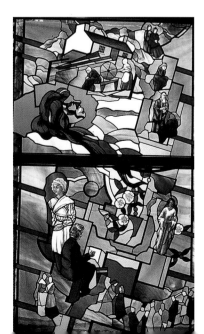

Design Sourcebook

STAINED GLASS

LYNETTE WRIGLEY

NEW HOLLAND

MARINE
LIFE

Some glass, especially when mouth-blown, has a flowing

surface texture which can capture the movement of the ocean

or the shimmering effect of light on the sea. The translucent

nature and brilliant colours of glass lend themselves

particularly well to nautical themes. From the tranquil tones of

aquamarine and intense, Mediterranean

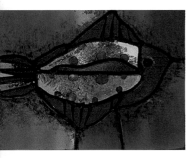

blues to more diluted hues of inland lakes

and rivers, the glass itself can inspire artists

to recreate the myriad effects of different

kinds of water and the living organisms of the deep.

◭ Fish panel. Danielle Hopkinson.
Painted and leaded panel. 15 ¾ x 21 ½ in
(40 x 55 cm). 1996

*The paintwork has added interesting
textures to the surface of the fish and
softened the outline against the blue
background, creating depth and tonal
changes. The metallic spots were cut from
brass and applied with adhesive.*

◖ The Field of Sunflowers (detail).
Jun Ishidoya. Etched, painted and leaded
glass. 72 x 42 in (180 x 105 cm). 1986

*Here, flashed glass has been etched to
varying depths, providing both a sharp
outline and subtle intensities of colour,
creating contours on the crab's body.*

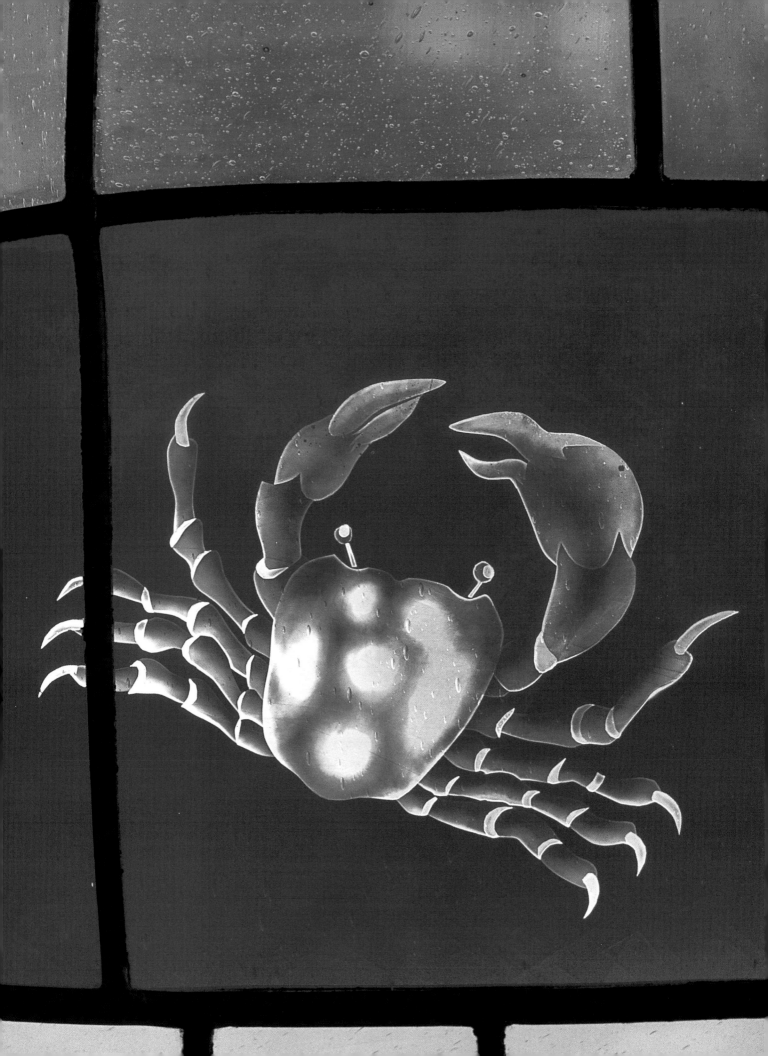

Noah's Ark (detail). Paul Quail. Painted and leaded glass. Overall size: 72 x 92 in (180 x 233 cm). 1996

The synthesis of outline and painting in this design for a private chapel in Norway creates a beautiful image. The entire window also features the native flora and fauna of that country.

Boat Roundel 3. Rowena Lewis. Painted and leaded glass. 19 ½ in (50 cm) diameter. 1995

Widely used in stained glass, the theme of a boat has been given a contemporary touch in this clever design. A spiralling cobweb of lead lines radiates from a guiding star. The central spokes become the ship's masts. The bold outlines of the details were created with tracing paint - the yellow and amber sections shaded with matt paint altering the colour tones and controlling the translucency of the glass.

Exhibition Panel. Jane Woodall/Kansa Craft.
Painted and leaded panel. 2 ft 6 in x 3 ft 6 in
(76 x 107 cm). 1994

*Made for a touring exhibition about the history of
domestic stained glass windows, this modern example
uses a background of blue and green streaky cathedral
glass. Iridized globules are incorporated into the
diagonal shafts of light.*

Pool Door. Randy Sewell. Laminated, painted and etched leaded glass. 36 x 20 in (90 x 51 cm). 1993

Antique and machine-rolled glass are combined into a unique design with subjects relating to the client. Likenesses of the family's hands are etched in a pattern reminiscent of Navajo friendship quilts.

Bathroom Window (detail). Anita Pate. Sandblasted, plated antique and float glass. Overall size: 51 x 27 ½ in (130 x 70 cm). 1994

The contoured, shell-like form created with sandblasting floats peacefully into vision in this soothing piece whose overall undersea effect is achieved by the directional feel of the images.

14

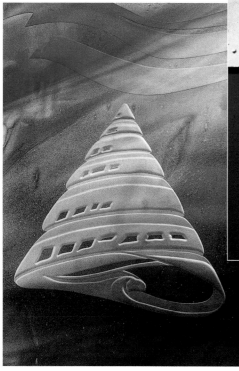

Aquarium. Mark Bradford/Ten & Six. Painted, stained, etched and leaded glass. 4⅞ x 28 in (12.2 x 70 cm). 1994

A kaleidoscope of colour sings out from this active and detailed underwater scene. Richly patterned corals and glowing red and orange fish emerge from a bed of dense underwater foliage.

Primary Ties. Linda Lichtman. Etched and sandblasted, painted and enamelled glass. 12 x 9 in (30 x 22.5 cm). 1992

Fish dive and snake across three separate pieces of glass threaded together with wire. The original manufactured colours have been imaginatively manipulated to produce the desired variations of hue, texture and colour density.

Seascape. Rosalind Grimshaw. Fused and leaded glass. 36 x 21 in (90 x 55 cm). 1995

Commissioned in memory of a lost child, this window has a soothing and mysterious presence. The yellows, blues and movement allude to the sea, a natural force at once healing and cleansing.

Waves. Caroley Bergman-Birdsall/Yn-Y-Wlad. Leaded glass in forged iron frame. Size of each panel: 62 x 22 in (157 x 56 cm). 1990

Using both machine- and hand-blown glass, the design for this screen was inspired by the colours and movement of the sea and the reflections of light playing through the ocean depths. The bold, sweeping curves of the waves pound across the triptych with great force.

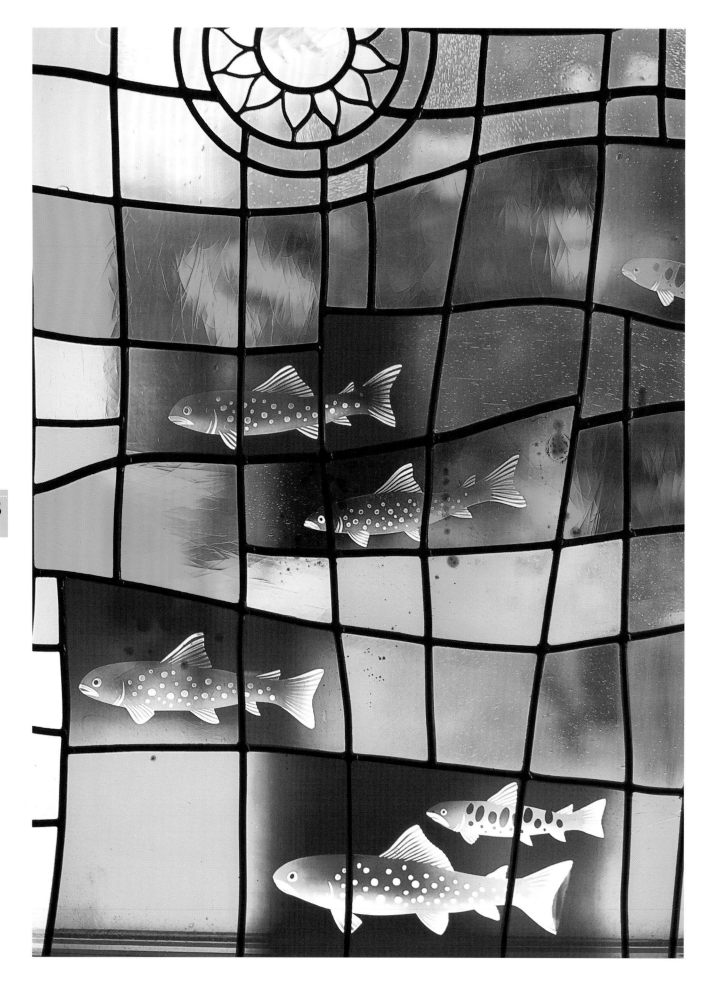

A Constellation of Summer: Andromeda (detail). Jun Ishidoya.
Etched, painted and leaded glass. 53 ½ x 17 in (149 x 43 cm). 1991

*In what he calls a "fantasy of space", this Japanese artist has used
textured glass to lend depth to the background. Lead cames delineate
the outline of the fish, and fine details are etched from the body and
fins of fish from his native Hokkaido.*

The Field of Sunflowers (detail).
Jun Ishidoya. Etched, painted and leaded
glass. Overall size: 72 x 42 in
(180 x 105 cm). 1986

*The lead cames contribute to the feeling of
the ebb and flow of water in this intensely
colourful window. Flashed glass of various
hues has been etched in varying degrees to
reveal subtle tonal changes.*

Tow Wings (detail). Jun Ishidoya.
Etched, flashed and leaded glass.
48 x 31 ½ in (120 x 80 cm). 1996

*In this close-up the superb artistry and
subtlety of the etched fish can be seen as
they appear to swim through the lead
lines and into the paler shafts of light.
The inspiration for Tow Wings came
from the writings of Rudolf Steiner.*

◗ **Seascape** (detail). Lydia Marouf. Etched, painted, stained and leaded glass. 20 in (50 cm) square. 1985

Aspects of coastal landscapes inspired this evocative work in which the colours, shapes and textures of rocks and shells mingle with the sky and sea.

◗ **Darwinian Salmon** (detail). Tony Banfield. Leaded glass. Overall size: 21 ft 5 in x 8 ft 2 in (6.5 x 2.5 m). 1994

One of the many images from a triangular window on a theme of Charles Darwin's Creation of the Species. The window also features butterflies, monkeys and birds of paradise.

Ammonites.
Frankie Pollak.
Sandblasted float
glass. 24 x 12 in
(60 x 30 cm). 1997

*This fascinating panel
was inspired by the
strong, spiral shapes
and textures of fossils.
The intricate pattern
was created with a
hand-cut stencil and
was sandblasted onto
float glass.*

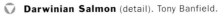

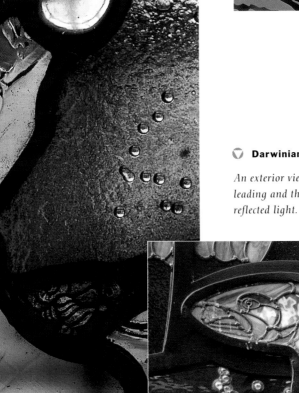

Darwinian Salmon (detail). Tony Banfield.

*An exterior view of the window, clearly showing the
leading and the colours of the opalescent glass as seen in
reflected light.*

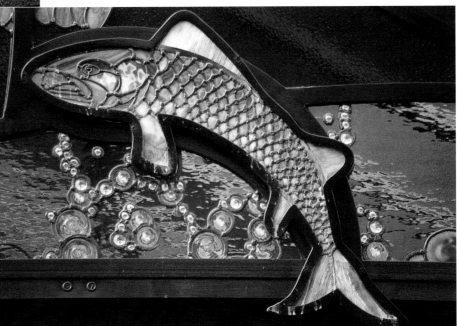

PEOPLE & PORTRAITS

Historically, most themes including figures in stained glass

were inspired by religion but in the present day, a diversity of

styles for capturing the human form has emerged alongside the

development of glass as a secular medium of artistic expression.

The depiction of people in glass is probably one of the greatest

challenges for contemporary artists, who are moving away from

classic representations while still using

traditional methods of painting and

staining. Glass painting is an exacting

art, however, and it is not necessary to make all figures

detailed. In some cases, the human form can be clearly defined

with outline and colour, shape and inflection.

⬤ **Images of Byzantium III: Weeping.** Caroley Bergman Birdsall/Yn-Y-Wlad. Etched, painted, enameled and leaded. 22 x 13 in (55 x 33 cm). 1992

Inspired by Byzantine sacred paintings and mosaics, this panel depicts the virgin Mary cradling the head of Jesus after the Crucifixion.

◐ **The Curse of Blodeuwedd I**. Gareth Morgan. Painted and leaded. 26 ¼ x 27 in (66 x 67.5 cm). 1994

The visual brilliance and translucency of mouth-blown antique glass is the "canvas" for this autonomous panel. The artist has created a stunning image as dramatic as the metamorphosis it depicts. One of a series inspired by Welsh mythology.

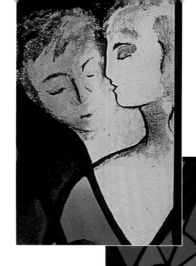

◁ **The Blue Window** (detail).
Patricia Clifford.

*Minimal paintwork was just enough to
define the faces.*

 **The Blue Window.** Patricia Clifford.
Mouth-blown glass, etched, painted and leaded.
41 ¾ x 29 in (107 x 74 cm). 1995

*Images emerge from a background of luminous
blues. The varied shades of antique flashed glass
were extensively etched to give subtle changes in
tone and light. The leadwork orchestrates the
movement and colour in this vibrant piece which
was inspired by the joy at the birth of a new baby.*

▷ **Front Door Panel.** Mollie Meager. Plated,
etched, stained and painted, leaded glass.
31 x 15 in (80 x 40 cm). 1995

*Made for a panel above a door opening onto a
narrow street, the design for this window is
energetic and uplifting and plays with
the movement in the sky outside. The suggestive
curves of the leading contribute to the impact
of the images.*

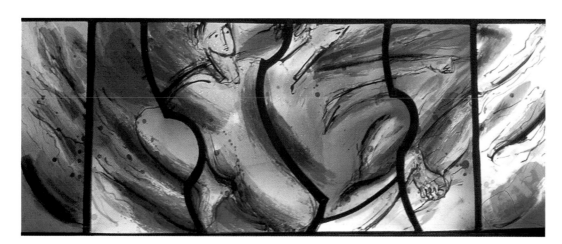

◗ **Stop!** Beverly Bryon. Sandblasted and leaded glass. 17 in (44 cm) square. 1994

Inspired by memories of vibrant colours and streaming sunlight during a visit to Maine one Fall, the artist chose to combine these influences with a sandblasted detail of her own handprint, enjoying the possible interpretations.

◗ **Heads.** Alan Stott. Cast and fused panel. 9 in (22.5 cm) square. 1997

This sculptural panel was made by first making a clay model into which impressions were made with children's toys. A plaster mould was taken and the glass was then cast into this shape and pieces of coloured glass fused on to it.

Jidai Matsuri. Paul Dufour. Etched, painted and leaded. 45 x 32 in (114 x 82 cm). 1982

An exotic, costumed figure is set against a colourful background in this piece inspired by the Festival of Ages in Japan. The glass globules on the head-dress were fixed with silicone and details on the costume etched off flashed antique glass.

Gandalf. Jude Tarrant/Sunrise Stained Glass. Etched, painted and silverstained glass. 24 ¼ in (61 cm) square. 1995

In blue flashed glass which has been etched and plated to red flashed, etched glass. the artist captures the moment in Tolkien's great work, The Lord of the Rings, when the great Doors of Durin open at last to that magical and elusive word, "friend".

Sebastian. Vital Peeters. Painted, enamelled, etched and leaded. 24 x 22 ¾ in (62 x 58 cm). 1994

Symbolic images combine to create a powerful narrative statement. St Sebastian is depicted as a gay icon, flanked by a skinhead and a priest. The triangle represents the Holocaust.

The Idiot. Garth Edwards. Leaded glass. 24 x 19 in (61 x 48 cm). 1984

One of many glass portraits created by this artist. In this case the piece was interpreted from an idle drawing.

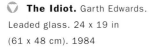

Hands (detail). Sue Woolhouse. Painted, stained and leaded glass. 9 ⅜ x 15 in (23.5 x 38 cm). 1994-5

Created at a student workshop given by Woolhouse, this piece bears the stamp of the individuals involved in making it and displays the skills of the artist and her exploration of how light behaves in a variety of painted surfaces.

Two Guys. Garth Edwards. Opal flash and clear glass with copper layer, lead came and brass bar. 12 x 24 in (30 x 60 cm). 1982

These amusing heads were the result of an experiment by the artist in which he cut out a thin layer of copper, "threw it in the woodstove overnight to patina and made a sandwich" - the layer of copper held in place between the clear and flash glass by lead came and reinforced by a soldered brass bar.

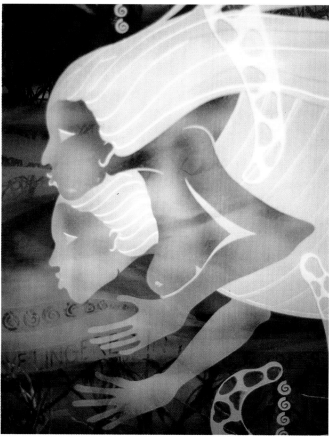

△ **Alice in the Flower Garden** (detail). Vital Peeters. Painted and enamelled glass. Overall size: 20 ½ in (52 cm) diameter. 1995

The subject appears to be suspended within the swirling, transparent, reamy glass. Coloured and black enamel paints highlight and animate both the girl and flowers in this leaded panel inspired by Alice in Wonderland.

◁ **Naiads** (detail). Anita Pate. Sandblasted, plated. 18 x 22 in (46 x 56 cm). 1995

A delightful evocation of water nymphs which forms part of a leaded panel. The streaky antique glass and the clear float glass have each been sandblasted and plated together for extra tonal depth.

School Activities. Sue Woolhouse. Etched, painted and leaded glass. 38 ¾ x 22 ¾ in (98 x 58 cm). 1996

For children, by children. Hearts, circles and crosses decorate this brightly coloured window which incorporates pictures by primary school children and was made up in the artist's studio.

Red Head with Green Eye. Linda Lichtman. Etched, painted and laminated. 13 x 10 ½ in (33 x 27 cm). 1992

A piece of glass has been transformed into an expressive image using acid etching and applied vitreous enamels. The piece is suspended by wire to hang like a glass painting.

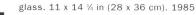

Journey to the East. Gaylene Allan-Richardson. Etched, painted and leaded glass. 11 x 14 ¼ in (28 x 36 cm). 1985

A compelling image portrayed in an expressive style. Etching, painting and shading have created variations in tone and line. The abstracted patterns decorating the rich, yellow glass work well with the harmoniously balanced colours.

30

100 Years of Soap Making
(detail). Lydia Marouf. Leaded, etched and painted glass. 21 x 13 in (60 x 36 cm). 1988

Another wonderful detail (see also pp 28-9) from this artist's commission in celebration of a commercial product and its packaging. The window is rich in content, and there is an interesting contrast between untreated areas of glass and the highly painted areas of layered images, colours and textures.

BIRDS & ANIMALS

Creatures from the animal kingdom have featured in stained glass for centuries, often appearing in church windows illustrating the lives of the saints. Biblical creatures were commonly found in nativity scenes, while heraldic panels included wild and mythical beasts. More recently, small decorative paintings of garden birds were common in Victorian domestic glass.

Birds and animals provide both delicate and dynamic shapes for artists, with intricate textures of fur or feather. Their colours can be muted or vibrant, and as in the past, they may be decorative or symbolic.

Owl and Swallow. Deborah Lowe. Painted, silverstained, etched and leaded. 19 ½ in (49.5 cm) diameter. 1991

The painted feathers of swallows in the summer sunshine and owls hunting by night represent the turn of the seasons and the transition from day to night in this design for a window in a converted barn.

Eurynome - the Star of the Sea. David Wasley. Layered and painted dichroic glass. 20 in (51 cm) diameter. 1997

One of three "star" windows including Puliar and Averimos, the morning and evening stars. Inspired by the Greek creation myth, it shows Eurynome, the Goddess of All Things, who rises from Chaos and assumes the form of a dove.

Tow Wings (detail). Jun Ishidoya. Etched and leaded glass. Overall size: 47 x 13 in (120 x 80 cm). 1996

The outstretched wings of the bird have been clearly defined at the tips by etching away the surface of the deep blue flashed glass. The subtle, contrasting colours are cleverly juxtaposed, providing layers of depth and tone.

Owl (detail from **The Time of Bloom in a Field**). Jun Ishidoya. Etched, painted and leaded glass. Overall size: 6 ft 2 ½ in x 4 ft 5 ¾ in (189 x 137 cm). 1987

One of many creatures in Ishidoya's large window depicting an aspect of his native Hokkaido. He combines areas of detail with large areas of space and colour and creates many images through extensive use of etching.

Bird (detail from **The Time of Bloom in a Field**). Jun Ishidoya.

Varying depths of acid etching have produced tonal changes in the flashed glass. The "stars" appear to shine brightly in the foreground and also gently fade away into the distance of the background colour.

Stag (detail from **The Field of Sunflowers**). Jun Ishidoya. Etched, painted and leaded glass. Overall size: 6 ft x 3 ft 6 in (180 x 105 cm). 1986

A majestic creature, his shape rendered in a faithfully realistic outline, with tonal changes outlining his form. The etched modulations of the blue, flashed glass background create a misty atmosphere.

Constellation of Summer: Andromeda (detail). Jun Ishidoya. Etched, painted and leaded glass. Overall size: 59 x 17 in (149 x 43 cm). 1991

This animal has a more abstracted nature than the clearly outlined stag, above. Dappled light from variegated circles etched off the glass contribute to the slightly mystical feel of this piece.

Bird (detail from **The Time of Bloom in a Field**). Jun Ishidoya. Etched, painted and leaded glass. 6 ft 2 ½ x 4 ft 5 ¾ in (189 x 137 cm). 1987

A reverance for Nature and a taste for aesthetic simplicity characterize this artist's work. Clearly singing its heart out, this small bird has been sensitively and beautifully executed.

Kingfishers. Michael G. Lassen. Painted, stained and leaded glass. 36 ¼ x 26 ¼ in (92 x 66.3 cm). 1992 *The vibrant colours of a pair of kingfishers in flight, set against their textured and varied environment, are beautifully combined and painted.*

Overleaf **Earth Animals** (detail). Sue Woolhouse. Painted, sandblasted and leaded. Overall size: 39 in (1 m) diameter. 1996

The stylized image of an ox sits amid an abstract display of colours, textures and mirror in this vibrant roundel now in the atrium of a college. The starting point for this design was the original use of the site for farmland which has now been built over.

◑ **Kingfisher** (detail). Ken Adams/Opus Stained Glass. Leaded glass. Overall size: 5 ft 10 in x 26 in (187 x 67 cm). 1996

In the foreground, flowing branches and elongated and curved leaves stretch languidly across the composition, while further back suggestions of water and downland make a suitable background setting for this beautiful kingfisher.

◐ **Rabbits.** Jude Tarrant/Sunrise Stained Glass. Painted, etched, stained and leaded glass. 26 x 13 ¾ in (61 x 35 cm). 1992

This window was commissioned for a young boy who wished for his favourite animals to be portrayed in glass. Fine brushstrokes faithfully reproduce the soft yet thick quality of the animals' fur, and the details of the fruit, flowers and insects are intricately painted.

FLORAL DESIGNS

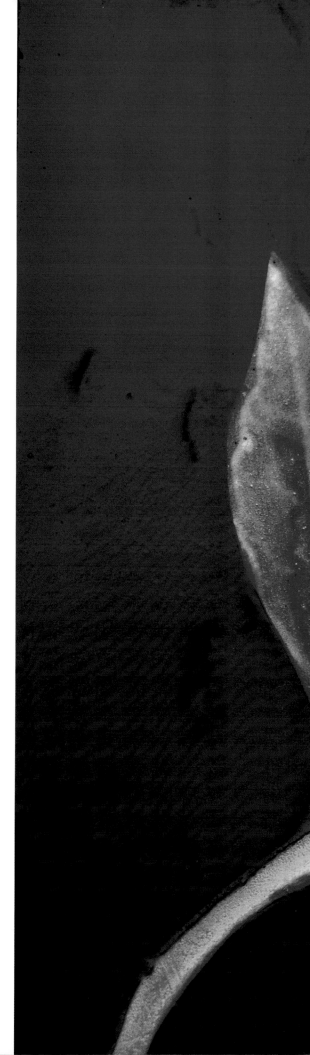

Designs inspired by Nature, especially flowers, are easy

to live with and are timeless. Years ago, the windows of

William Morris echoed his love of organic forms, and

Louis Comfort Tiffany's windows were

abundant with such images. In

contemporary stained glass,

interpretations of these themes are more

varied than ever, and the individual

styles of artists reflect their distinctive approaches, from

stylized to realistic. The rich variety of colours available

in glass can inspire exquisite floral designs imitating

the hues of both wild and cultivated flowers.

Springtime (detail). Lydia Marouf. Etched, painted and stained glass.
Overall size: 6 ft x 18 in (190 x 50 cm). 1996

*An innovative composition using the vibrant colours of irises, poppies and
other early flowers.*

Rose (detail). Sue Woolhouse. Slumped glass. Overall size: 8 in (20 cm)
square. 1995

*One of a series of floral windows capturing the intricacies of flower and leaf
in a classic colour combination of rich red and yellow.*

The Tree of Leaf and Flame. Wolfe van Brussel/Mirage Glass.
Coloured glass and copper foil. 18 in (45 cm) diameter. 1992

*The animated shapes and lively colours of this design were
inspired by a Welsh story in which a tree, at once both green
and burning, leads to the Celtic underworld.*

Day Lilies. Randy Sewell. Copper-
foiled antique and opalescent glass.
30 x 18 in (75 x 45 cm). 1990

*With its Arts and Crafts feel, this
realistic representation of traditional
lilies is created from a mixture of
opalescent glass set against a
background of clear antique. The
elegance of the lily is captured in
various stages of development, from bud
to full bloom.*

42

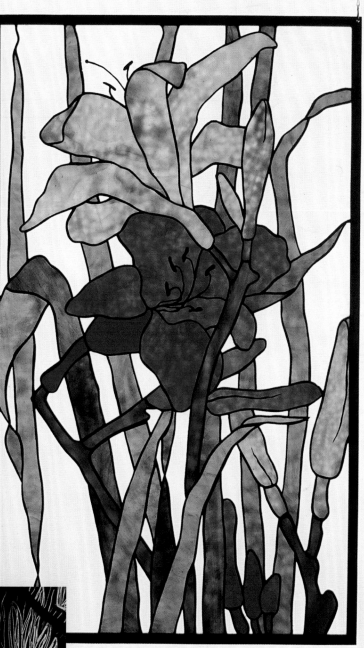

Border Scratchboard (detail). Linda Lichtman. Etched,
painted and leaded antique, flashed, stained glass.
22 x 18 in (55 x 45 cm). 1988

*Shapes evoking the natural world have been scratched out of
paint applied to the glass surface. The narrow lines reveal
the colour of the glass beneath, which glows through the
dark background.*

Flowers. Peter Allen. Etched, stained, painted, gilded and leaded panel. 26 x 16 in (65 x 45 cm). 1992

This artist has a free and painterly style. Here, the inherent regularity of the lead cames is diffused with free-flowing paintwork which softens any potentially sharp contrasts of colour.

Sunflowers. Helen Robinson/Oriel Stained Glass. Leaded glass. 45 x 24 in (115 x 60 cm). 1996

Strong images of positive and cheerful sunflowers make a compelling design commissioned for a memorial window from a watercolour by Ron Jolly. The window incorporates translucent, semi-opaque streaky and cathedral glass.

Anemones (detail). Sue Woolhouse. Etched, painted and leaded glass. Overall size: 30 ⅜ x 31 ¼ in (76 x 78 cm). 1994

The colours and shapes of these vividly coloured flowers are exquisitely portrayed here. To emphasize the desired effect of an intense, jewel-like quality, Woolhouse surrounded the central panel with textured, opaque, black glass.

FLORAL DESIGNS

Plants in a Window. Linda Lichtman. Enamels on sandblasted and leaded float glass. 17 x 14 in (43 x 36 cm). 1990

Here, Lichtman has transformed clear glass into a tapestry of soft colours. She was inspired by the sight of a row of plants, placed side by side as if observing the world, in the window of a house.

Leaf Litter. Cedar Prest. Leaded glass. 20 x 31 in (50 x 80 cm). 1989

Inspired by things Australian - the light, the land, the soft, grey greens, yellows, purples - this window contains a fascinating mixture of materials. Amidst the variety of antique glass, there are some three-dimensional pieces made by the artist.

Hospice Window. Virginia Hoffman. Sandblasted and leaded glass. 6 x 4 ft (180 x 120 cm). 1994

This window has a deliberately meditative quality, appropriate to its setting, and the colours were chosen for their overall calming effect. This artist favours surface treatments such as sandblasting, relishing the added dimension gained and the real design quality achieved. The apparent symmetry of the design alters unexpectedly in the area of the leaf-like forms.

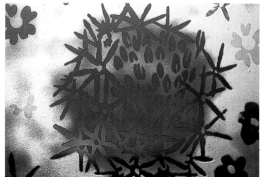

Allium (detail). Sue Woolhouse. Sandblasted and stained glass. 8 x 6 in (20 x 15 cm). 1994-5

One of a series of windows whose theme is the seasons of the year. The spikiness of the onion flowers has been cleverly and innovatively captured.

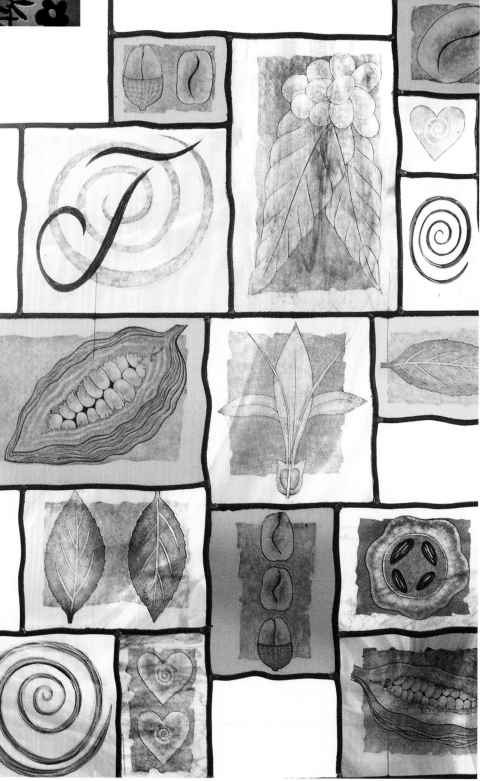

Thornton's Café
(detail).
Danielle Hopkinson.
Painted, slumped and
leaded glass. Overall size:
47 x 24 in (120 x 60 cm).
1997

*Taken from a large panel
on a theme of tea, coffee
and chocolate, the leaves,
beans and pods used in
their production are
painted in warm
coordinating tones of
amber and brown. Clear
float glass has been
slumped and loosely
painted into impressions of
spiralling motifs.*

Mayals (detail).
Rhiannon Morgan. Sandblasted,
acid-polished and leaded glass.
13 ⅝ x 33 ¼ in (34 x 86 cm).
1991

*The shapes of the leaves are
variegated in both style and
emphasis on this background
of float glass. This is one of a
series of panels combining
traditional and modern
elements and techniques.*

Motifs. Lynette Wrigley.
Sandblasted and leaded flashed
antique glass. 19 x 31 in
(47.5 x 77.5 cm). 1997

*Here I used sandblasting
both to abrade and partially
remove the surface colour of the
glass to create a variety of
images, including geranium
leaves, doodles and fruit, on a
pattern of square and
rectangular shapes.*

ABSTRACT DESIGNS

THERE IS A GREAT FREEDOM and vitality in abstract designs for stained glass, whether they are created as architectural decoration or autonomous panels. Non–figurative themes are sometimes difficult to define and

can be elusive in meaning. They may include elements derived from figurative sources or be patterns of light in structured or fluid compositions, exploiting the colors and textures of the medium, or a personal expression of the artist.

Gwreiddiau. Gareth Morgan. Stained, painted and leaded glass. 20 ⅜ in (5.09 cm) diameter. 1989

An autonomous panel, inspired by the root of a rose bush which the artist dug up in his garden and whose shadow created interesting shapes. He has used a variety of techniques with mouth-blown antique and clear cathedral glass.

DNA Galaxy. Paul A. Dufour. Sandblasted and leaded glass. 48 x 32 in (123 x 81 cm). 1980

A colourful comparison between our galactic environment and the microscopic detail of genetic material. The center circle is fused glass and the scattered glass globules have been attached by the artist with silicone.

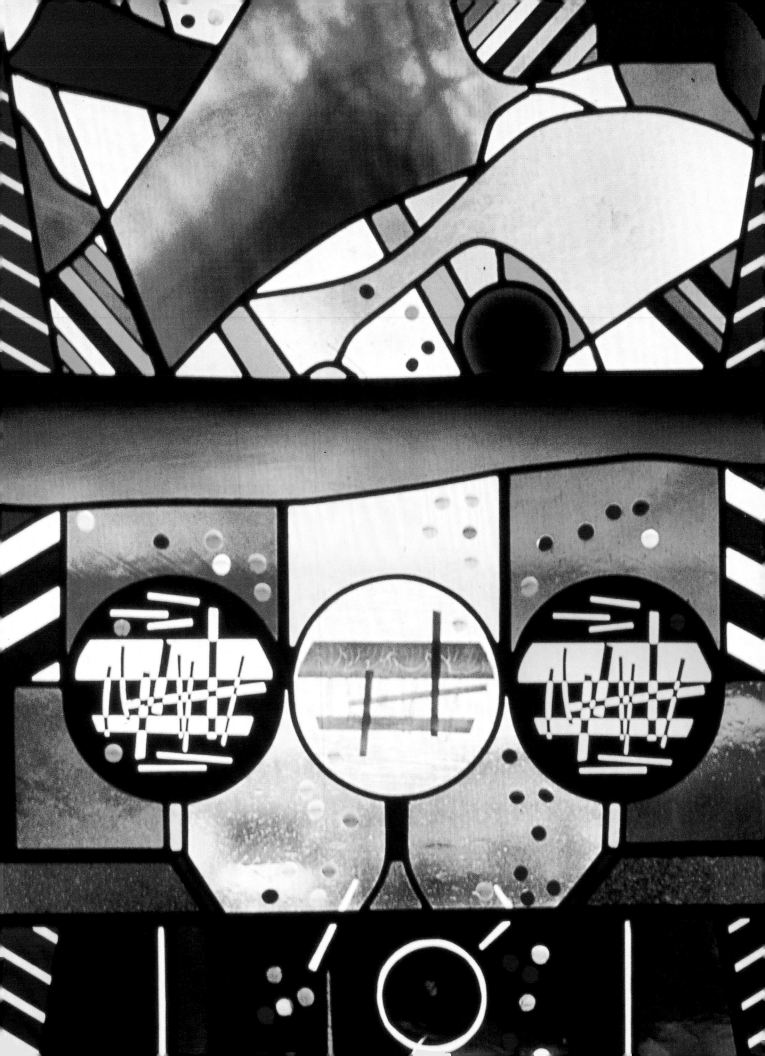

Genesis/RFK (detail). James B. Furman. Leaded glass. 12 in (30 cm) square. 1997

An interpretation of a tree of life, this is one of six sections created for a public art commission in New York. The raised detail panel is centred on a smaller, square, bevelled glass jewel. Zinc and lead cames were used and the window is installed in a polished aluminium frame.

Enamelled Tablet with Etched Border. Linda Lichtman. Sandblasted, etched, painted and enamelled. 14 ½ x 11 in (37 cm x 27.5 cm). 1990

Evoking the natural world, the layers of organic shapes in soft, smoky colours are "framed" by the translucent border. Float glass has been sandblasted, acid-etched, painted and enamelled and incorporates a former glass printing plate.

Sculptural Panel (detail). Alan Stott. Kiln-formed cast glass. 9 in (22.5 cm) square. 1997

To create this ethereal, elusive piece, the artist first made a clay impression using combs, from which a plaster mould was made. Glass was then placed onto the mould and fired at high temperatures to melt it and fill the indentations.

⬡ **At Last!** Mark Angus. Acrylic, glass and leading. 31 in (80 cm) square. 1983

The design for this autonomous panel for a Swiss exhibition was derived from some paper collage work the artist had already worked up. Shapes have been cut from a single piece of acrylic into which the stained glass and lead were skilfully inserted.

◗ **Library Window** (detail). Ed Carpenter. Etched and painted glass, grid, copper, marbles, in sealed double glazed panel. 19 ft x 19 ft 6 in (5.8 x 5.9 m). 1993

"Technical but traditional" and "wired to the past" are phrases the artist uses to describe the window he created for the library at the University of Wisconsin in Madison. 750,000 glass marbles were included in the design which comprises 56 sealed panels.

New Landscape. Linda Lichtman.
Etched, silver-stained, flashed glass and
painted and enamelled float glass.
10 x 15 in (25 x 38 cm). 1995

*A "glass painting" inspired by the natural
world. Flashed and float glass have been
transformed by the artist using a variety
of different techniques.*

The Wet Land (detail). Linda Lichtman. Etched, painted, enamelled, stained and laminated glass with caste bronze rods. 2 x 22 ft (60 cm x 20.9 m). 1993

A source of light and life for the editorial offices of the New England Journal of Medicine, this piece evokes marshland, full of life, always renewing itself and ever growing.

Spiral Structure no.1. Linda Lichtman. Etched and leaded flashed glass. 32 x 15 in (85 x 38 cm). 1992

One of a series of spiral structures inspired by the landscape of America's Southwest. This artist is interested in the tension between her organic use of colour and line and the strict grid elements of the glass shape. The pieces of glass are loosely held together with wire threaded through perforations in the panels and tied to the rectangular frame.

Day/Night Panel no.8. Linda Lichtman. Etched and pierced glass and copper. 13 x 3 ½ in (33.2 x 9 cm). 1996

From an exhibition entitled "structures and images", these glass pieces were suspended from the ceiling using wire. During the day transmitted light brings the stained glass to life, while by night, the patina of the metal is vibrantly colourful.

55

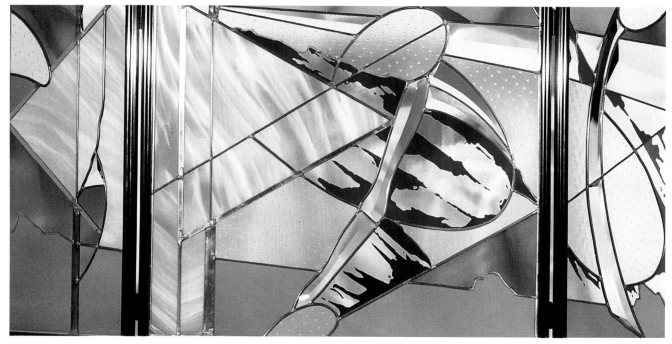

◗ **U. C. L. A. Humanoid.** Dick Weiss. Opaque leaded glass. 2 x 5 ft (61 x 152 cm). 1980

Inspired by the time he taught summer school at the famous California campus, the artist chose geometrics to suggest the human form in this almost three-dimensional piece which appears suspended in space and time.

◖ **Impressions on a Wave.** Virginia Hoffman. Etched and leaded glass. 45 x 72 in (114 x 186 cm). 1995

One of three leaded panels forming a fire screen. The aim of the artist was to create the effect of collage which she achieved by combining different textures, unusually-shaped bevels and an impression of torn paper in the etched glass.

Gordian Knot. Paul A. Dufour. Etched and leaded glass. 50 x 22 in (160 x 55 cm). 1980

Referring to the ingenious knot of bark cut by Alexander the Great with his sword in the 4th century AD, this window uses a combination of flashed antique glass and some double flashed (colour on colour) glass, which allows light of different hues to flow through the etched lines.

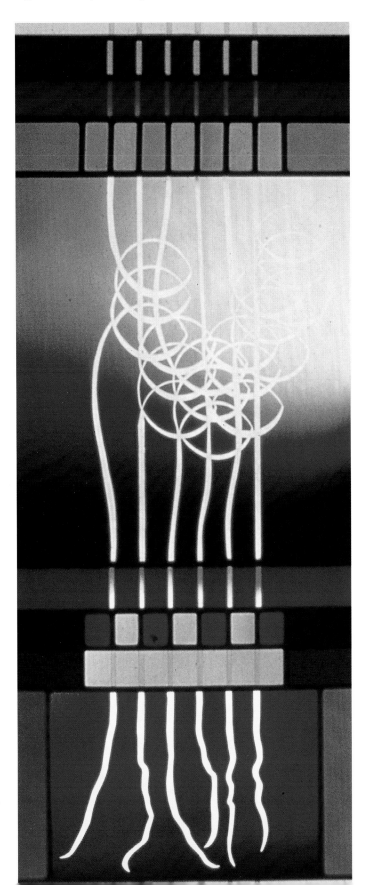

ABSTRACT DESIGNS

Door for Richard Bruehl. Dick Weiss. Leaded glass. 6 x 2 ft (183 x 61 cm). 1991

A composition on a theme of diamonds, snakes and roundels for the door of a private residence. The handblown roundels are intersected with angular pieces of yellow opalescent glass in a diagonal formation.

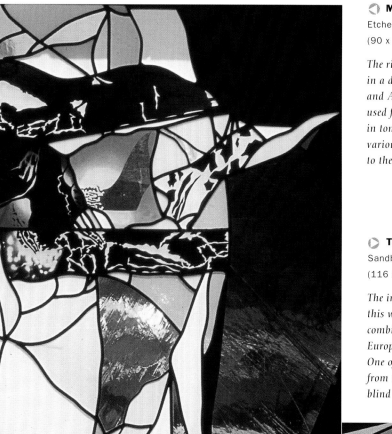

◀ **Mountain Pass I.** Paul A. Dufour. Etched and leaded glass. 36 x 34 in (90 x 85 cm). 1984

The richness of a hidden valley is reflected in a design combining European antique and American cathedral glass. Dufour has used feather-etching to create graduations in tone and has employed lead cames of various widths which have become integral to the design.

▶ **Teiresias II.** Paul A. Dufour. Sandblasted and leaded glass. 46 x 34 in (116 x 86 cm). 1993

The intense activity and richness of colour in this window were achieved with a combination of sandblasted, flashed European antique glass and coloured acrylic. One of two windows depicting the conversion from chaos to order, and referring to the blind soothsayer of Greek mythology.

▶ **Ionic Transformation.** Paul A. Dufour. Leaded glass. 36 x 34 in (90 x 85 cm). 1992

A variety of widths of lead lines "draw" an abstract theme expressing the crucifixion and the Holy Trinity. European antique and English Hartley Wood mouth-blown antique glass have been used here.

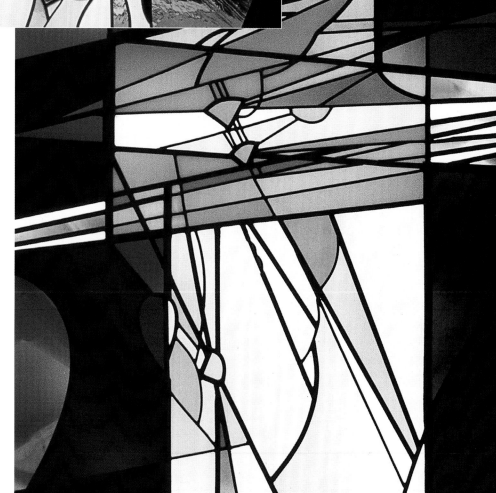

We, Too, are Stardust. Rhiannon Morgan.
Painted, etched and leaded glass. 28 x 30 in
(70 x 77 cm). 1996

*A window containing a witty play on words and
reflecting the celebrity couple who commissioned
it for their private residence. An attractive
combination of streaky antique glass, opalescent
glass, painted and clear lenses.*

◐ **Windblown Thistle.** Brian Berg. Russian flashed white antique and opalescent leaded glass. 34 ¼ in (87 cm) diameter. 1987

Inspired by the client's favourite artwork, a Chinese brush painting of a thistle blowing in the wind, the very functional purpose of this attractive piece was to screen telegraph poles from view outside the window.

▽ **The King of the Traffic Lights.** Jonathan Butler. Leaded glass. 30 x 18 in (80 x 50 cm). 1988

Sympathetic to the aperture into which the window was to fit, this panel was designed with no constant angles or structured dimensions.

▽ **To Mary.** Molly Meager. Etched, silver-stained, plated and leaded glass. 24 x 36 in (61 x 92 cm). 1994

Words from a poem by John Clare chosen by the client were used freely as a design element in this window for a dining room. The shapes were inspired by a pebble found on a beach in Greece.

◐ **Elements.** Stuart Low. Painted, stained and etched glass. 15 in (38 cm) diameter. 1997

One of two windows occupying a natural stone setting which playfully combine a theme of the four elements with the celestial. The dark outlines of the lead cames enhance the vividness of the colours.

Strata (detail). Yolanda Harry. Etched, stained, silk-screen painted, leaded glass. 39 in (100 cm) square. 1996

This piece, on a theme of crude oil, organic matter and mechanics, was designed for an oil company. The lead lines, an integral part of the composition, are decorative rather than merely functional.

Overleaf: **Southampton Waves** (detail). Ellen Mandelbaum. Silk-screen painted, leaded glass. 21 x 46 in (53 x 117 cm). 1989

Smoky opalescent and painted glass coalesce in an impression of waves in this detail of two windows for a summer home. Inspiration for the design came from the waves of the nearby sea and from stylized Japanese wave paintings.

Front door panel (detail). Lydia Marouf. Etched, painted, stained and leaded glass. 6 ft 7 in x 20 in (200 x 50 cm). 1996

Accentuated by the lead and paint work, the enlarged floral forms are stylized into rythmic dancing formations. Both Hartley Wood English streaky antique and Lambert's German antique glass were used in this window for a private residence.

Acorns and Branches. Di Green. Painted, plated sandblasted and leaded glass. 9 ft 7 in x 2 ft 3 ½ in (300 x 70 cm). 1991

A series of five panels making up an architectural mural which draws on small natural forms for inspiration. Glass, lead and paint flow together, the definition of the lead cames diffused by spontaneously varied brush strokes.

Acorn I (detail). Di Green.
Painted, plated and leaded
glass. 19 ¾ x 27 ½ in
(50 x 70 cm). 1991

*Line, colour and form merge
with sandblasted details plated
onto the back for extra depth in
this section from one of five
panels. Some pieces were painted
and fired three times to achieve
different densities of colour.*

Macaw. Emma Micklethwaite. Silk-screen painted, enamelled and leaded. 34 ¼ x 14 ¼ in (87 x 36.5 cm). 1996

Designed for an exhibition entitled "Jeweled Light", this abstract piece is elusive in meaning, yet visually very powerful. The paint was applied to the glass using silk-screen, which resulted in a tactile surface texture.

Internal window. Mollie Meager. Etched, painted, stained, plated and leaded glass. 24 in (61 cm) square. 1995

The abstracted image of a cockerel in vividly bright colours, inspired by the work of Marc Chagall, is central to this piece. Plating has extended the colour vocabulary and washes of silver stain add shades of golden yellow and amber.

ABSTRACT DESIGNS

Celestial. Stuart Low.
Painted, etched and leaded
glass. 15 x 11 in (38 x 28 cm).
1996

*One of two windows
commissioned for a natural stone
setting. Here, the artist created a
playful theme combining the
four elements with the celestial.*

Water. Beverly Bryon.
Leaded and sandblasted glass.
72 x 41 in (184 x 103 cm). 1995

*Inspired by a lifelong love of water, its
movement, translucency and ever-
changing character, the artist has
created a non-pictorial image using
mouth-blown glass and fluid lead
lines with sandblasted surface details.*

Marina. Lindsay Hughes/Cut 'n' Edge Stained Glass. Painted and leaded glass. 18 in (46 cm) diameter. 1996

Inspired by sailing vessels, portholes and ideas relating to maritime history, this artist often takes ideas from natural sources as a starting point for her inspiration and then creates abstractions from them.

Covenant. Elizabeth Devereaux. Handblown, flashed, etched and painted glass. 9 ft (2.75 m) square. 1994

The prism at the centre of this window represents the rainbow, the symbol of the covenant between heaven and earth, and between God and mankind.

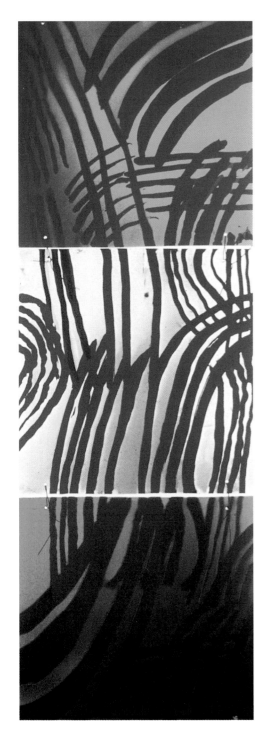

Line Drawing. Linda Lichtman. Etched, flashed antique glass. 24 x 8 in (60 x 20 cm). 1996

One of many autonomous pieces in this artist's repertoire of glass "paintings" which use acid etching both to subtract and reveal colour.

Robins Residence. Michael Davis. Etched, leaded and painted glass. 5 ft 7 in x 27 in (170 x 69 cm). 1991

Reminiscent of the traditional mihrab motif used in oriental rugs, the border was etched and painted using silk screen printing. The window was inspired by the Moorish architecture of the Alhambra in Granada, Spain. The blue in the keyhole symbolizes sky.

Collector's Door 2 (detail). Ellen Mandelbaum. Layered, painted and leaded glass. 28 in x 6 ft 3 in (75 x 187.6 cm). 1996

Incorporating two layers of painted glass, this attractive window allows the landscape beyond to be clearly seen. The juxtaposition of glass and view is an integral element in this artist's work.

Kites and People (detail). Sue Woolhouse. Painted, sandblasted and leaded glass. 15 x 9 ¼ in (38 x 23.5 cm). 1994

A collaborative window, made by the artist and young students of varying abilities, this entrance panel reflects the various aspects of the their lives, including shapes derived from a local kite festival.

◐◑ Rings of Power: Wititj and Wik. Marc Grunseit. Kiln-formed glass and stainless steel. 27 ¼ in (63 cm) diameter. 1997

Based on imagery sacred to the landscape and myths of the Australian aborigines, this gloriously colourful piece seems almost like a floating landscape of Australia, tethered to its origins by the penetrating, cold steel of modern life.

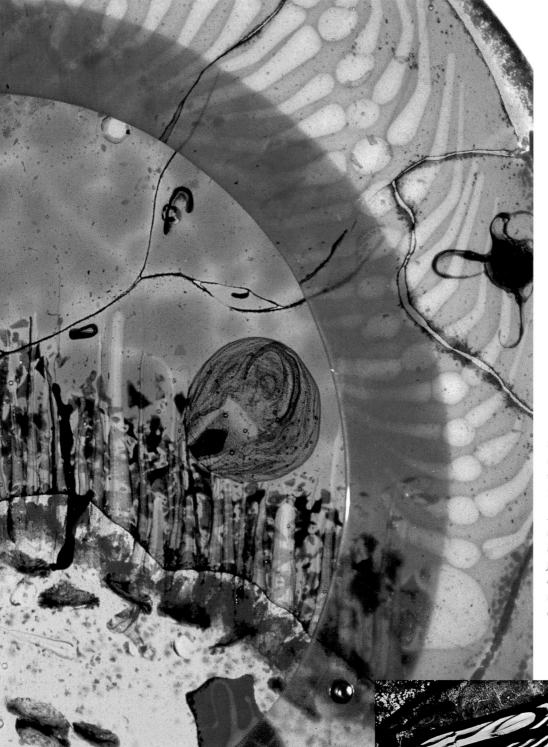

⬙ Patterns in Paint 2.
Rowena Lewis. Painted,
stained and leaded glass.
9 x 11 in (23 x 28 cm).
1995

*A panel inspired by the
many effects which can
be achieved using paint on
float glass. The artist used
a variety of implements
to produce this array
of patterns.*

ABSTRACT DESIGNS

Red Wheat (detail). Ellen Mandelbaum. Painted glass. Overall size: 30 x 57 in (76 x 145 cm). 1991

The artist was inspired by the extraordinary power of colour and paint in the design for this piece. This section from a large window entitled "Wales Landscape" displays her painterly, abstract brushwork.

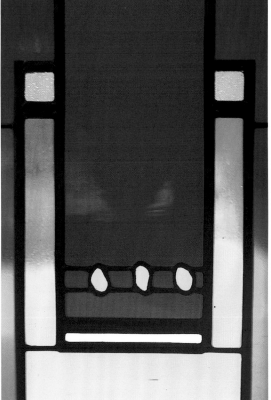

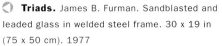

Bath (detail). Mark Angus. Leaded glass. 47 x 59 in (120 x 150 cm). 1979

The strongly graphic effect provided by the leading is an integral part of the design for this window, which is one of a pair of door panels for a private residence. Glass in primary colours is assembled within different widths of lead. The oval shapes of yellow glass provide small jewels of colour within the rectangular composition.

Triads. James B. Furman. Sandblasted and leaded glass in welded steel frame. 30 x 19 in (75 x 50 cm). 1977

Inspired by memories of the classic Wurlitzer juke boxes with their slabs of coloured glass, this artist used plate glass and prism glass pieces mounted over coloured antique glass.

Teiresias. Paul A. Dufour. Sandblasted, etched and leaded glass. 48 x 30 in (120 x 80 cm). 1993

Just as order was anticipated to come from chaos in the ancient Greek prophecy upon which the inspiration for this design originated, so an organized, geometric symmetry emerges in flashed glass from the influx of fluid and random structures below.

▶ **River Glass.** Bronwen Jones. Copper-foiled panel. 10 x 12 in (25 x 30 cm). 1994

This autonomous piece ingeniously incorporates fragments of Victorian domestic glass which were included as found. The centre was pieced together like a jigsaw using copper foil, since the glass pieces varied in thickness .

▶ **Aranda Window.** Cedar Prest. Painted, enamelled, stained and leaded glass. 7 ft 11 in x 17 ft 1 in (240 x 520 cm). 1987-8

Derived from a painting depicting three stories from the Australian Dreamtime, this piece evoking their sacred lands was a community project made with the help of aboriginal Aranda women at an arts centre in Alice Springs.

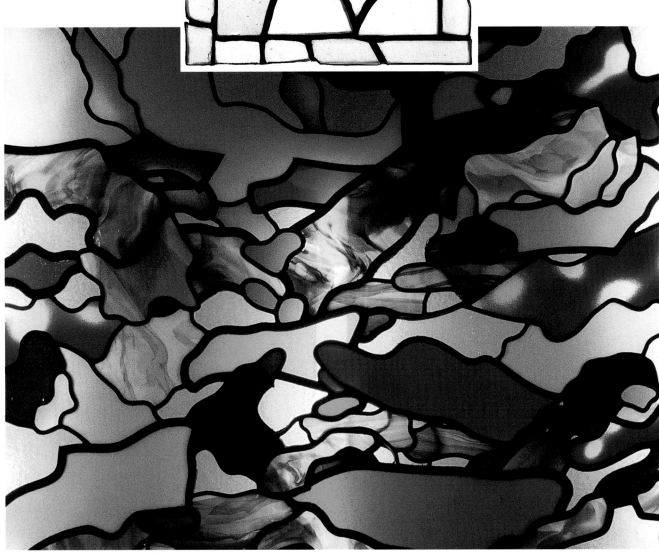

◆ **Wilken Residence.** Michael Davis. Leaded, stained, sandblasted and layered antique glass. 30 ½ x 32 ½ in (77 x 82 cm). 1996

Inspired by the shimmering, ever-changing quality of water, the artist has created overlapping organic shapes in streaky and flashed glass, their outlines emphasized with varying widths of lead.

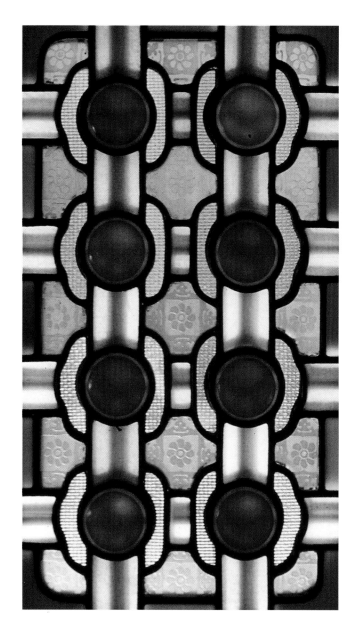

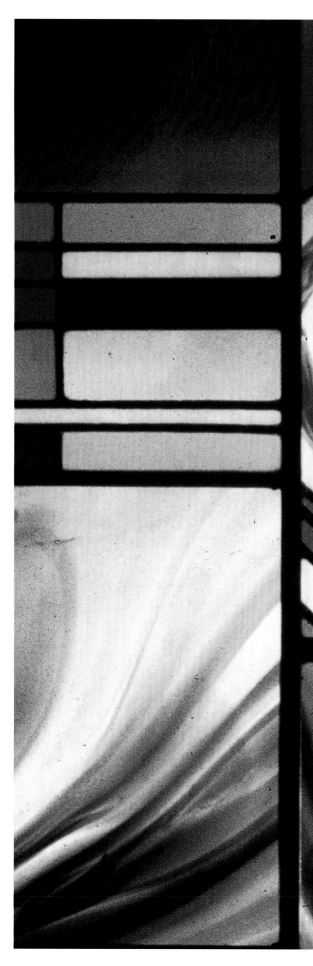

Hi-tech Lace.

James B. Furman. Leaded glass
and mirror. 14 x 26 in
(36 x 66 cm). 1993

*This double panel, which can be
viewed either in reflected or
transmitted light, successfully
blends old and new materials,
including mirror.*

The Winds of Saturn.
Paul A. Dufour. Leaded glass.
42 x 24 in (107 x 61 cm). 1978

Inspired by the artist's interest in astronomy, the beautiful smoky swirls of the Hartley Wood streaky antique glass have been incorporated sympathetically into a design based on the idea of the planets.

ABSTRACT DESIGNS

Moon Sonata.
Paul A. Dufour. Leaded glass.
36 x 40 in (91 x 102 cm). 1973

Spherical shapes and harmoniously balanced colours produce an almost ethereal luminosity. The music of Beethoven was the inspiration for this piece.

◐ **Spots.** Anji Marfleet/Through the Looking Glass. Leaded mouth-blown glass and agate. 11 x 21 in (28 x 53 cm). 1995

This window shows off the indefinable beauty of Hartley Wood mouth-blown glass, which the artist combined with the natural patterns and hues of agate to create a kaleidoscope of colour.

◐ **Three Rondell Windows.** Dick Weiss. Leaded mouth-blown roundels. Size of each panel: 2 x 6 ft (61 x 183 cm). 1995

These stunning roundels were mouth-blown by Sonja Blomdahl and skilfully incorporated into windows for the chapel of a clinic.

Symphony (detail). Paul Quail. Leaded and painted glass. 4 x 7 ft (122 x 213 cm). 1988

Part of a French window using mouth-blown Hartley Wood glass. The inspiration for this design came from the notion that each individual has a vocation in life just as each instrument in an orchestra plays a part in a classical symphony.

ABSTRACT DESIGNS

○ **Private residence.** Beverly Bryon. Leaded and mouth-blown glass, bevelled glass pieces.
5 ft x 5 ft 9 ½ in (152 x 176 cm).
1994

A window with a contemporary, abstract feel, whose lattice work echoes Charles Rennie Macintosh's famous "ladderback" chair. The formality of these sections is complemented by the circles and curves in the remaining areas. The fluidity of the mouth-blown glass meanders through the lead and wood lines, adding softness to the piece. The wooden frame is an integral part of the design.

○ **Mountain Calligraphy.** Paul A. Dufour. Etched and leaded glass. 31 x 48 in (79 x 122 cm). 1984

This window is one of a series by the artist inspired by mountain passes and his reaction to passing through the darkness of a crevasse. It incorporates both American and European antique glass and etched flashed glass.

The Creation of Blodeuwedd. Gareth Morgan. Leaded, sandblasted and painted. 22 ½ in (56.5 cm) square. 1993

This autonomous panel is one of a series in a private collection inspired by the story from Welsh mythology of the transformation of a girl into an owl.

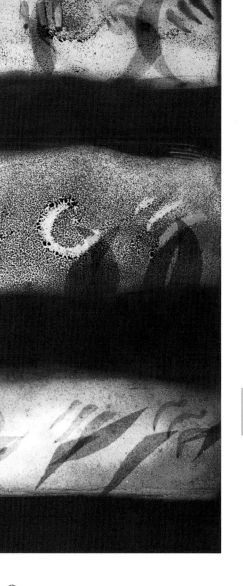

My Blue Heaven. Clare Sinclair. Etched, sandblasted, enamelled, plated and laminated glass. 20 x 14 in (51 x 36 cm). 1996

Here the artist has created sensitive images using a combination of techniques and incorporating four layers of glass.

Landscape Fragment.
Linda Lichtman. Etched, painted and
stained flashed glass. 9 ½ x 10 in
(24 x 25 cm). 1991

*The artist liked a piece of glass she
had previously rejected from another
panel and decided to use it as the
new "canvas" on which to create a
glass painting. One of many of this
eminent American artist's
fascinating glass canvases.*

Alexander. Paul A. Dufour.
Antique and flashed glass and clear
acrylic. 48 x 32 in (122 x 81 cm).
1980

*The artist has used contrasting
widths of lead with angled overlays.
Characteristic of this artist's work the
colours used are powerful (and
balanced), taking full advantage of
the purity and brilliance of colour
stained glass offers.*

The Red Tree. Dick Weiss. Enamelled and leaded glass. 6 x 4 ft
(183 x 122 cm). 1986

*The artist has created textures and detailing using enamel paint and a
variety of different glasses in brilliant colours to create an intriguing
and lively piece.*

NON-SECULAR DESIGNS

ALTHOUGH STAINED GLASS is no longer exclusively

an ecclesiastical art form, many windows continue to be commissioned

for religious buildings, old and new. The need for non–denominational

windows provides artists with the opportunity to express their individual

styles in both abstract and figurative designs. While stained glass with a

religious theme may be featured elsewhere in the book, this chapter also

includes work created especially for, and sited in, sacred buildings.

◭ Water and Wheat (details). Ann Sotheran. Painted, stained, etched and leaded. 5 x 7 in (12.5 x 17.5 cm). 1996

Two of four single lights for a hospice chapel. The sheaves of corn shown top right represent "the bread of life", one of the basic sacraments.

◗ Fisher of Men (detail). Ann Sotheran. Painted, stained, etched and leaded. 16 x 68 in (40 x 170 cm). 1995

Part of the east window in All Saints, Cleveland, which depicts Christ as a fisher of men. A fresh and uplifting effect is achieved through the use of colour in this celebration of life which includes animals, plants, fishes and people. The ox is the symbol of St Luke.

◖ **Choir Window** (detail). Mark Angus. Silkscreen on glass.
51 x 37 in (130 x 95 cm). 1996-7

*A detail taken from a sample panel or test section for a church window
whose inspiration was a 15th-century painting by Van Eyck. Paint has
been silk-screened onto glass to which silver stain was added to create
an aged look reminiscent of the original.*

◖ **St John.** Wolfe van Brussel/
Mirage Glass. Painted, stained and
leaded panel. 7 ½ x 10 ½ in
(19 x 27 cm). 1994

*This small, leaded piece, a museum
study, is a copy of a 14th-century
German panel, the original of which
is in Strasbourg. It reflects the
traditional approach to figurative
imagery of that early period.*

St George. Danielle Hopkinson. Leaded, painted and etched glass. 30 x 12 in (80 x 30 cm). 1994

In this panel, one of six windows for a private dwelling, featuring saints of specific importance to the client, the figure of St George is traced by the lead cames. A limited colour palette and economy of paintwork contribute to the clarity of this graphic image.

93

NON-SECULAR DESIGNS

Saint Mary the Virgin, Manchester Cathedral (detail). Tony Hollaway. Painted, etched and leaded. Overall size: 20 x 10 ft (6.7 x 3 m). 1980

Pulsating with colours and textural images, this window combines non-figurative and symbolic images. It continues the ancient tradition of non-secular glass painting in a contemporary language on a tapestry of abstraction.

◯ **Shavuot.** Robert Pinart. Leaded and painted glass. 24 x 48 in (61 x 122 cm). 1993

Carefully selected, mouth-blown flashed opal antique glass was painted on easel in the studio. Congregation Ahavath Israel, Kingston, N.Y.

▽ **Holy Ghost window.** Diether F. Domes. 13 ft 3 in (400 cm) diameter. 1993

This design uses the dove not as a traditional representation or symbol of the Holy Ghost, but presents the moment of immersion of the dove's wing movement into the waters of baptism, i.e. into the earthly domain of God. Mission Church, Karslruhe.

Baptism Window (detail). Ann Sotheran. Painted, etched and leaded. 18 x 54 in (45 x 135 cm). 1995

Animated with light, clear areas of glass have been imaginatively etched, including the hovering dove of the Holy Spirit, with the seven gifts of the Spirit lettered on the glass below. From the left-hand light in St. Mary's, Middlesborough.

The Calling of St Peter.
Paul Quail. Painted and leaded.
Each light: 20 x 80 in
(50 x 200 cm). 1989

A memorial window in Sweffling, Suffolk, in which a young man, depicted as St Peter in contemporary dress with a boat, is being beckoned by Christ to join him. The detailing is beautifully clear - note how the painted waves gradually recede as ocean meets sky.

The Great Catch.

Eva Sperner-Zernickel.
Sandblasted, leaded, clear and
flashed glass.
11 ft 10 in x 39 in
(360 x 100 cm). 1993

*One of six windows about the
life of St Peter. St Petrus,
Mühlbach.*

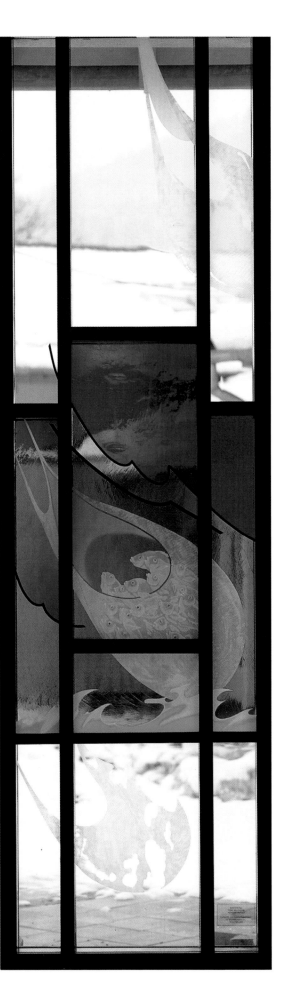

Fount of Wisdom and Rocks.

Paul Quail. Painted and leaded.
10 x 48 in (25 x 120 cm). 1986

*With the fount of wisdom representing
priesthood, and rocks, the Church, a
palette of soft colours fills the length of
this window with sparkling light.
Langham Carmel, Norfolk.*

NON-SECULAR DESIGNS

Pilgrimage. Clinton Alexander. Painted, etched and leaded panel. 48 x 30 in (124 cm x 78 cm). 1996

Inspired by the artist's visit to Ethiopia, this panel depicts Coptic priests with decorated umbrellas proceeding to Beta Ghiorghis church in Lalibela, Ethiopia.

Timkat. Clinton Alexander. Etched, painted and sandblasted, leaded panel. 48 x 24 in (120 x 60 cm). 1996

The festival of Epiphany being celebrated amid the rock churches of Ethiopia, symbolizing the harmony between heaven and earth, God and Man. The top row of figures has been etched from a single piece of flashed glass.

Beta Gheorghis.
Clinton Alexander. 36 x 24 in
(90 x 60 cm). Sandblasted,
flashed and mouth-blown antique
glass, painted and leaded. 1996

*Taking the shape from a window
at the Beta Ghiorghis church in
Ethiopia, the artist has used a
Coptic "ceiling of angels "as his
inspiration for the design of the
central area. Ruby flashed glass
represents the red cloth which
covers the Ark of the Covenant.*

African Chief. William Fraser Lowe.
Painted, etched, silverstained and leaded
window. 32 x 50 in (81 x 127 cm). 1997

*Although this artist specializes in the
restoration of medieval windows, he
relished the challenge of this commission
for a family mausoleum in Kenya.*

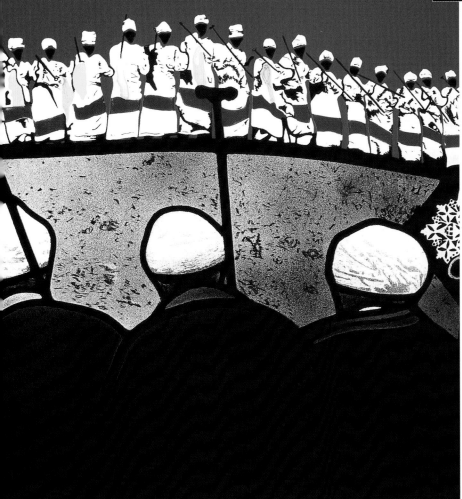

NON-SECULAR DESIGNS

Swifter than Eagles, Stronger than Lions.
Ruth Taylor Jacobson. Painted, etched and leaded antique glass.
39 ½ x 23 ½ in (100 x 60 cm). 1993

*The title for this piece derives from a Hebrew
inscription over the carved wood doors
of an old Cracow synagogue: "Be
strong as a leopard and swift
as an eagle, fleet-footed as a
stag, bold as a lion".*

Celebration. Ruth Taylor Jacobson. Painted, etched and
leaded antique glass. 39 ½ x 24 in (100 x 61 cm). 1994

*A powerful piece in which the faces and figures
were inspired by memories of a Sabbath
meal in Prague which, for this artist,
represented spiritual survival
and optimism.*

105

Night and Day.
Surinder Hayer Warboys.
Etched, painted, plated,
stained and leaded. 41 x 44 in
(104 x 112 cm). 1995

*This non-denominational
window for a hospice chapel
shows to great effect the way
this artist uses colour to play
with movement and stillness,
space and light. Specially
milled lead cames were used
for the assembly.*

NON-SECULAR DESIGNS

The Holy Spirit Window. Paul A. Dufour. Leaded glass. 54 x 30 in (21.6 x 12 cm). 1993

The inspiration for this window, the left portion of a dyptich, derives from the idea of purity in the wilderness. University United Methodist Church, Baton Rouge, LA.

The St Patrick Window. Paul A. Dufour. Leaded glass.
8 x 12 ft (2.4 x 3.7 m). 1975

A flowing, serpentine form threads through this composition of diagonal and horizontal lines. Three circles in the centre represent the clover leaf which, with the serpent, are attributes of this saint. St Patrick's Church, Lake Providence, LA.

The Presentation of Jesus at the Temple.
Rowena Lewis. Painted and leaded glass. 26 x 23 ½ in
(67 x 60 cm). 1996

*Here the artist has chosen to reproduce a medieval window as
a means of studying traditional techniques. Her study of a
twelfth-century Bible window in Cologne Cathedral gives us
an insight into the iconographic imagery and decorative style
of the period.*

Hanukkah. Ruth Taylor Jacobson. 23 ¼ x 17 ¼ in
(71 x 43 cm). 1993

*Here, a golden candelabrum, the menora, which is
traditionally lit during Hanukkah, the Jewish Festival of
Lights, rises out of dark blue into clear blue light. Its
branches bear the symbols of Life and Hope, found in
carvings from old synagogues and ancient coins.*

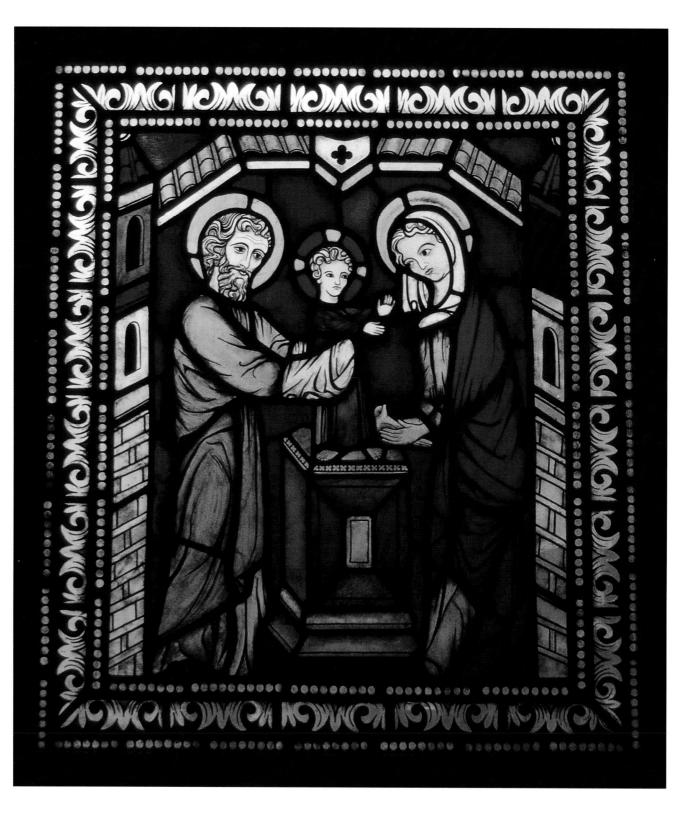

Mother and Child. Stuart Low. Stained, painted and leaded glass. 18 x 30 in (46 x 76 cm). 1993

Low wanted to recreate the quality of a charcoal and ink drawing on white paper using vitreous paint on glass. This autonomous panel was made for a competition and incorporates antique and water glass.

Fisher of Men (detail). Ann Sotheran. Painted, stained, etched and leaded glass. 68 x 16 in (173 x 41 cm). 1995

A detail from the east window of a northern England church depicting Christ as a "fisher of men", catching the whole world in the net of his teachings and ministry.

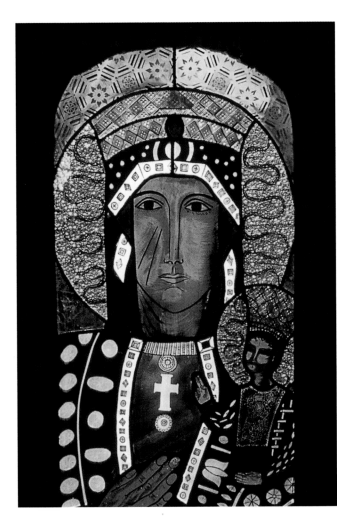

Gilbert White Memorial Window. Jude Tarrant/Sunrise Stained Glass. Painted, etched, stained and leaded. Centre light: 16 ft x 30 in (4.9 m x 76.2 cm); left and right lights: 14 ft x 24 in (4.3 m x 60 cm). 1993

Commemorating the 200th anniversary of the death of the naturalist Gilbert White, this window portrays the flora and fauna of his celebrated classic, The Natural History of Selbourne.

The Black Madonna. Anji Marfleet/Through the Looking Glass. Painted, stained and leaded glass. 42 x 15 in (75 x 38 cm). 1995-96

This powerful portrait is based on a painting, reputedly by St Luke, of the Virgin Mary, which was stolen from the Polish Church in the 15th century. It was eventually retrieved, damaged, and here the artist has faithfully translated the original into glass, even including the "scars" on her face.

Our Lady of Felicity (detail). Paul A. Dufour. Painted and leaded. 11 x 9 ft (3.4 x 2.7 m). 1975

A design influenced by Notre Dame la Belle Verrière. Here Dufour created a feminine figure of slender proportions, the folds and details of her robes defined by line and colour, her head-dress adorned with glass globules.

NON-SECULAR DESIGNS

Ruth Taylor Jacobson. Painted,
etched and leaded antique glass.
Three panels: 24 x 8 ¾ in,
38 ¼ x 25 ¼ in, 24 x 11 ½ in
(60 x 22 cm, 96 x 63 cm,
60 x 29 cm). 1995

*This artist takes inspiration
from the lives of her ancestors,
and the glorious and tragic
history of the Jewish people. A
printmaker and painter, her
technique with creating stained
glass is first to acid-etch the
glass to create a textured surface
before rubbing in the paint.*

Creation of the Universe (detail). Michael G. Lassen. Copper-foiled opalescent glass. 53 ⅜ x 41 ½ in (135.2 x 104.4 cm). 1996

Three panels of a window in the Roman Catholic Church at Hinckley, Leicester, representing the big bang theory of the creation. The world is depicted as a ball of fire with the atmosphere and the elements being formed.

Prophesy Window. Robert Forman. Copper-foiled glass. 170 x 24 in (442 x 60 cm). 1991

Commissioned by Temple Emau-El, Bayonne, NJ, this biblical window represents the words of Ezekiel 36: 35 - the transformation of the land from desolation to a new life.

◐ **Memorial Window** (detail). Gareth Morgan. Painted, leaded and sandblasted. Overall size: 6 ft 3 ¾ in x 14 ¾ in (191.7 x 36.7 cm). 1996

A lancet window inspired by Psalm 148: a song of praise to God the Creator from the various aspects of his creation. Featuring a variety of painting techniques, the sections with their melodious colours and textured details have been sandblasted on the reverse, before being painted and fired. The border is a tinted Danziger glass.

Fishers of Men. Caroley Bergman-Birdsall/Yn-Y-Wlad. Painted and leaded. 6 ft x 2 ft 9 in (183 x 84 cm). 1993

A beautiful design sparkling with shimmering movement and imagery. Amongst the fish are handspun roundels representing the souls of men being "netted" in the murky depths and carried up towards the light of salvation.

East window (detail). Ann Sotheran. Painted and leaded. 19 x 65 in (48 x 169.8 cm). 1996

This part of the main East window represents wheat, "the bread of life", and also includes part of the crown of thorns which encircles the whole of this beautifully "layered" composition.

◗ **"I am the Vine"** (detail).
Cedar Prest. Leaded, painted and etched glass. 7 x 9 ft (2.1 x 2.7 m). 1973

Part of a Baptistry window depicting Christ as the source of all living waters and showing the sea, full of tiny organisms, behind which rise the crucified flames of the Holy Spirit.

⬡ **The Ark and the Rainbow.**
Paul Quail. Painted and leaded glass. Size of each panel: 18 x 10 in (45 x 25 cm). 1980

On a theme of living water, these lights for a Catholic church depict the receding waters of the Flood, with Noah's Ark resting on Mount Ararat, alongside the rainbow and the dove.

Ship of Souls. Val Green. Etched, painted and leaded.
13 ft 1 in x 9 ft 6 in (4 x 2.9 m). 1997

*The non-denominatinal design for this crematorium window
incorporates roundels and faceted jewels to represent souls. The
mast of the ship echoes the shape of a cross.*

Growth. Paul Quail. Leaded and painted glass. 51 x 18 in (128 x 45 cm). 1995

In this lancet window for a country church, softly coloured organic shapes are gently painted in fine detail, their forms animated with contrasting light and shadow.

Baptism. Paul A. Dufour and Samuel J. Corso. Leaded and painted glass. 24 ft base x 18 in peak (7.3 m base x 46 cm peak). 1997

The abstract design for this window for a Catholic church in Baton Rouge, LA., is in sympathy with the modern architecture of the building. The theme of waters flowing from the God-head is expressed in the rich colours and intense configuration.

🔺 **Deep Calls to Deep.** Gareth Morgan.
Etched, sandblasted, plated, painted and
leaded glass. Lancet size: 6 ft 2 in x 1 ft 5
in (188 x 47.3 cm). 1991

*The details for this double lancet memorial
window were either sandblasted or acid-
etched through the layer of flashed glass.
Its biblical theme was inspired by Psalm
42, verses 7-8: "Deep calleth unto deep at
the noise of thy waterspouts: all thy waves
and thy billows are gone over me."*

123

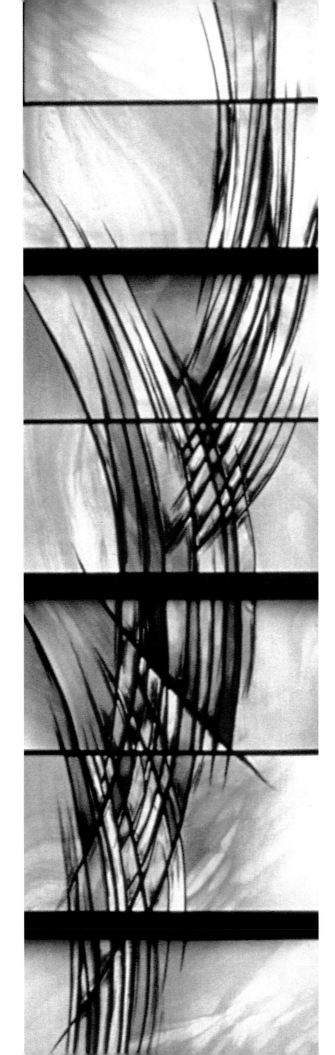

The Beat of Wings (detail). Elizabeth Deveraux. White on clear streaky mouth-blown glass. Painted, stained and leaded. 350 sq ft (106 sq m). 1996

Suggestive of feathers and wings, the patterns have been spray-painted onto mouth-blown, white translucent streaky glass to create a free-form, watercolour effect. The top layer of paint was fired with 24-carat gold lustre which is reflective at night.

Window No. 5 (detail). Ellen Mandelbaum. Painted and leaded glass. 8 x 3 ft (240 x 90 cm). 1995

A detail from one of ten windows in the sanctuary of a chapel. Vertical bands of creative details echo the parallel lines of glass in this beautifully balanced composition which combines both translucency and transparency.

Put in for the Deep (detail). Elizabeth Devereaux. Etched and leaded antique and layered flashed glass.
Overall size: 1000 sq ft (92 sq m). 1994

Colours combined with the strident sweep of lead cames cascade into a melody of movement and light. The title refers to the request Jesus made to his disciples after fishing all night.

NON-SECULAR DESIGNS

GLOSSARY OF STAINED GLASS TERMS

Acid-Etching Most commonly used on *flashed glass*, this treatment uses hydrofluoric acid to remove the thin layer of colour on the flashed glass, either completely or partially. It can create a softer and more delicate effect than sandblasting, but must be used with great caution.

Acid polishing A method whereby a solution of acid is applied to a non-reflective area, such as a sand-blasted image, to soften and add a brilliance and clarity to its surface.

Antique glass Mouth-blown, flat glass, with natural textures and striations. Each piece may be different with colours ranging from pale tints to rich tones.

Bevels Polished glass shapes with angled edges.

Cames Strips or lengths of metal with grooves on either side for inserting the glass. Usually lead, but can also be made of zinc or brass.

Cartoon The working drawing or blueprint for the design onto which the window is made.

Casting A process of heating pieces of glass in a kiln until it melts into a mould, or of pouring molten glass into a mould. The mould is usually plaster but glass can also be cast using the "lost wax" technique.

Cathedral glass Transparent, machine-rolled glass with an even surface texture. There are many other types of rolled glass.

Copper foil Used to join pieces of glass together. Most commonly used on internal or highly intricate windows requiring very small pieces of glass. Copper foil is also very useful when making sculptural pieces and lampshades.

Danziger glass Similar to *reamy glass*.

Dichroic glass A thin, highly processed glass treated with metal oxides. Dichroic glass changes colour according to the viewpoint of the onlooker.

Enamels Vitreous colours used to paint on glass which become transparent when fired in a kiln.

Etching A technique for removing or abrading the surface of glass using hydrofluoric acid or sand-blasting.

Firing Vitreous or enamel paints applied to glass which is fired in a kiln to fuse the paint to its surface.

Flashed glass *Antique glass* with a thin layer of colour on the surface. The base is usually clear but can also be of another colour. The top layer can be *sandblasted* or *etched* away to reveal the glass below.

Float glass Flat, clear sheets of machine-manufactured glass.

Fusing The process of heating different colours and pieces of glass until they become "soft" enough to bond together.

Kiln-formed glass Glass that has been *cast, slumped* or *fused* in a kiln.

Laminated glass Two layers of glass bonded together with resin.

Leading The term refers to the technique of assembling a window with lead *cames* to hold or join pieces of glass together.

Lenses Circular pieces of cast glass.

Lusters Paints with metallic iridescence.

Matting The creation of shade and tone when painting on glass. The initial layer of paint is partially removed using brushes or sticks (or any implement that suits the individual) to create highlights, textures and other effects.

Mouth-blown glass Glass made by using a traditional method whereby molten glass is blown into a cylindrical glass bubble call a "muff". Also referred to as hand-blown glass. The ends of the muff are cut off and the glass cylinder is split open along its length before being put back in the kiln where it unfolds into a piece of flat glass.

Opalescent glass Opaque glass of varying density, usually machine-made.

Paint Black or brown vitreous paints used for *tracing* and *matting* glass before it is fired in a kiln.

Plating Two pieces of glass placed together within a lead *came* to create different colours and layered effects.

Prisms Pyramid-shaped, cast *bevels*.

Reamy glass *Antique glass* with a flowing surface texture.

Resist A mask or stencil usually made from a sticky-backed material that adheres to and protects selected areas of glass during *sandblasting* and *acid-etching*.

Rolled glass Machine-made flat glass.

Roundels Machine-pressed or hand-spun circles of glass with rounded edges.

Sandblasting A treatment where sand is projected by a compressor onto the surface of the glass to abrade or penetrate it, producing an effect of deep "carving".

Silver stain A transparent colour which stains clear and pale tinted glass in shades from yellow to amber. It contains silver nitrate and penetrates the glass when fired in a kiln.

Slumped glass A sheet or piece of glass that is heated until it becomes soft enough to sink into a mould.

Tracing Lines painted onto glass with trace paint which is usually black or brown.

INDEX OF ARTISTS

The artists featured in this book are listed here in alphabetical order. The pages on which their work appears follow each entry. Their work is coded according to the following categories:

P: Public commissions
Pr: Private commissions
R: Restoration work undertaken
S: Suppliers (materials, tools, glass)
W: Workshops

127

128

Acknowledgments and photography credits

The Sunflowers on p. 43 are based on a water-colour design © by Ron Jolly.

Photography by the artists with the exception of the following:

Greg Andersen 52-53; Martin Avery 62t, 68-69; Jon Bouchier/New Holland (Publishers) Ltd 25b, 47b, 50b, 80t; Tessa Bunney 121r; Jo Burnes 86t; Douglas Cape 70; Malcolm Crowthers 32-33; Saari Forray 124r; Robert Foster 112; Anne Furman 50t, 78b, 82l; FXP Photography 109; Jeffrey Goldman 117r; Clifton Hall 72b, 125; Hatter Photographics 122-123; Victor Hugo 24b; Kansa Craft 13; Don Lawson 102, 103, 114-115; Lead & Light 99tr; Lincolnshire Life 94-95; Oliver Link 72t; Bruce Martin 17; Bob Ure 26b, 37b; Doug van Zande/Elizabeth Devereaux 124l; Wheelmark Studios 95; Dave Williams 27mr, 29b, 38-39, 40-41, 43b, 46t, 75; Helmut Zernickel 97m.

This edition published in 2002 by
New Holland Publishers (UK) Ltd
London • Cape Town • Sydney • Auckland
www.newhollandpublishers.com

Garfield House
86-88 Edgware Road
London W2 2EA
United Kingdom

80 McKenzie Street
Cape Town 8001
South Africa

Level 1, Unit 4, 14 Aquatic Drive
Frenchs Forest, NSW 2086
Australia

218 Lake Road
Northcote, Auckland
New Zealand

ISBN 1 85974 035 9

Editorial Assistant: Anke Ueberg
Designer: Grahame Dudley

Editorial Direction: Yvonne McFarlane

2 4 6 8 10 9 7 5 3 1

Artists on pp 2-7: p. 2 Deborah Lowe, p. 4 t Chloe Buck, m Jude Tarrant/Sunrise Stained Glass, b Gareth Morgan, p. 5 t Lydia Marouf, m Opus Stained Glass, p. 6 m Anita Pate, b Gareth Morgan, p. 7 t Linda Lichtman, b Lynette Wrigley.

Reproduction by Modern Age Repro House, Hong Kong
Printed and bound in Singapore by Tien Wah Press (Pte) Ltd